Ralph

by elaine morrison

series: Time, space,

all you need is 8.

first publishing Toronto, Canada 2011
ISBN 978-0-9739682-7-9

Ralph is volume 1 in the *Time, space, all you need is 8* series depicting philosophy on the meaning of life.

Ralph is a picture book featuring truthful events in the lives of Ralph (dog), George (cat), Elaine Morrison, and friend Shadow (black dog) in Toronto, Jerusalem, and British Columbia- although Ralph does disclaim any incidence of himself parachuting.

Time, space,
all you need is 8.

Ralph

by Elaine Morrison

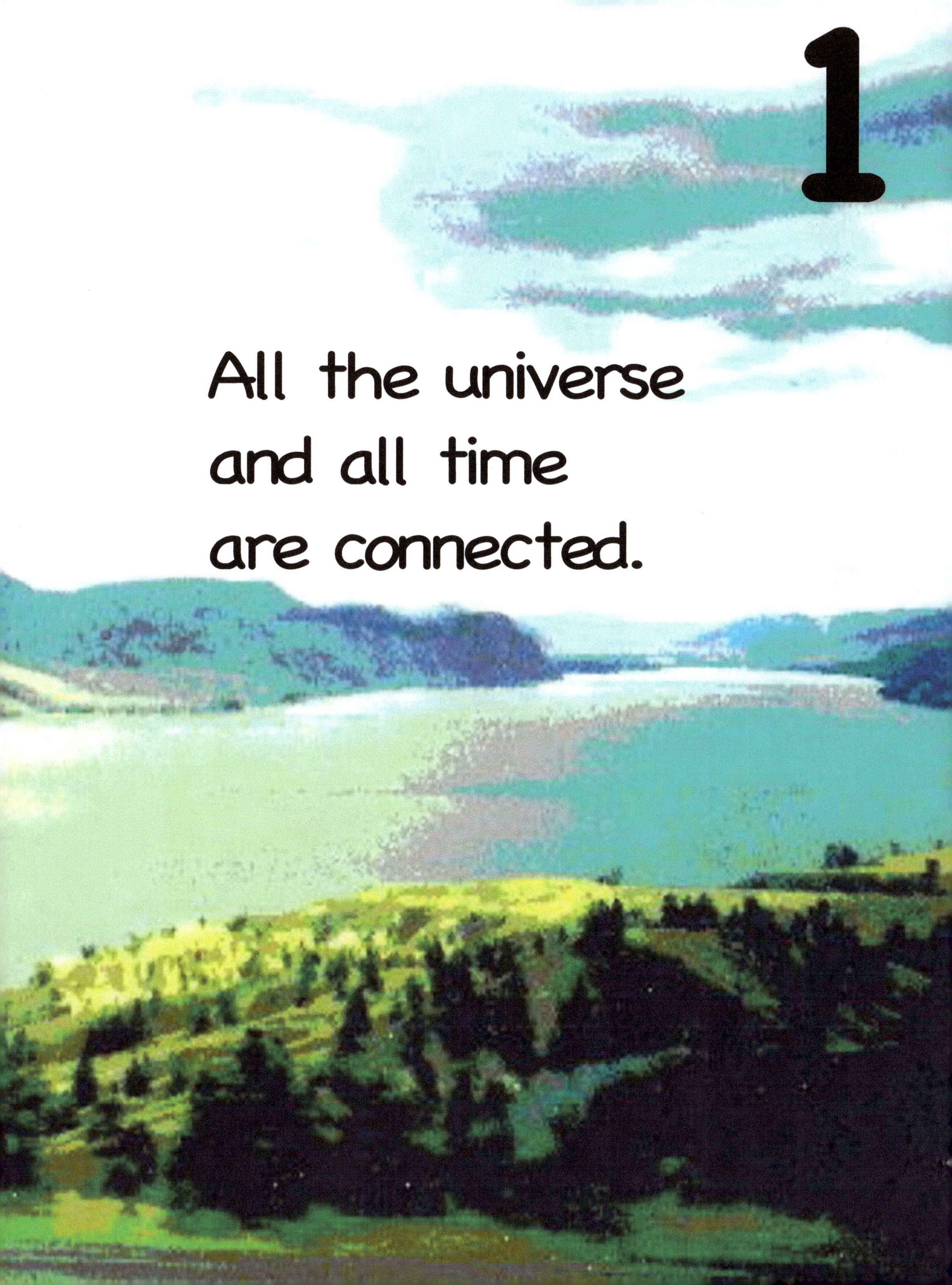

1

All the universe
and all time
are connected.

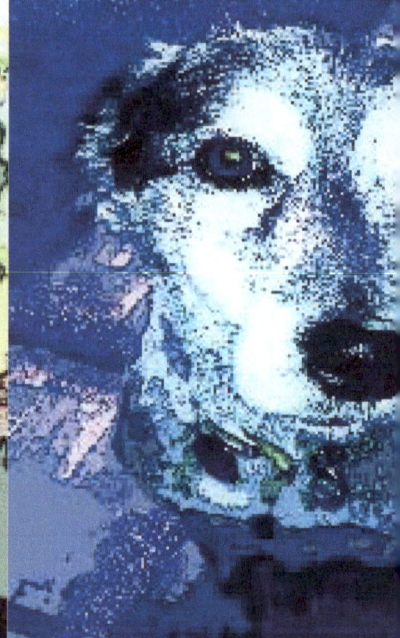

2

Although
any form
is possible,

the
universe
chose
to
become
Ralph
the
dog.

George the cat
knew,
and wished
for a friend.

5

So Ralph
came down

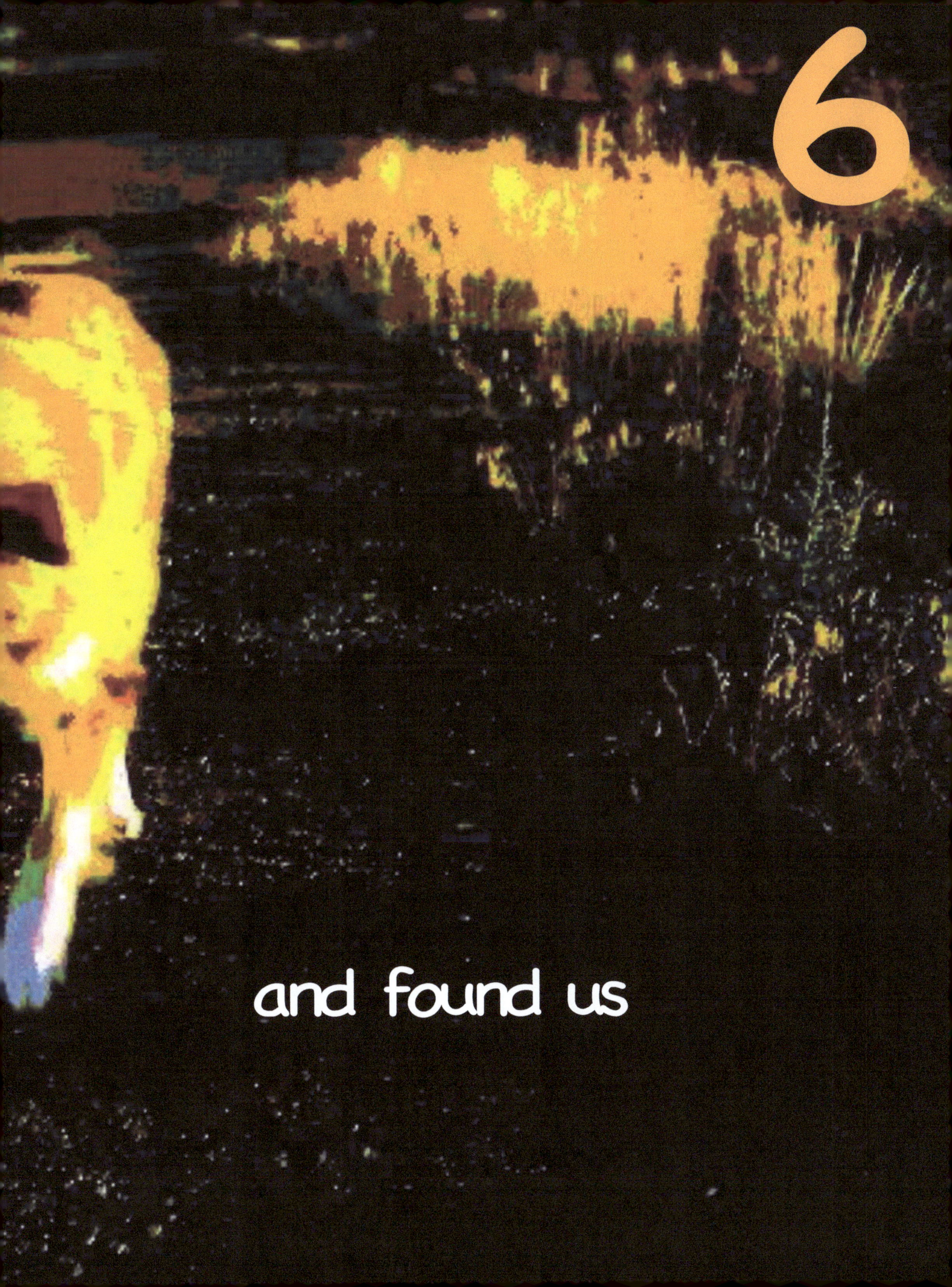

and found us

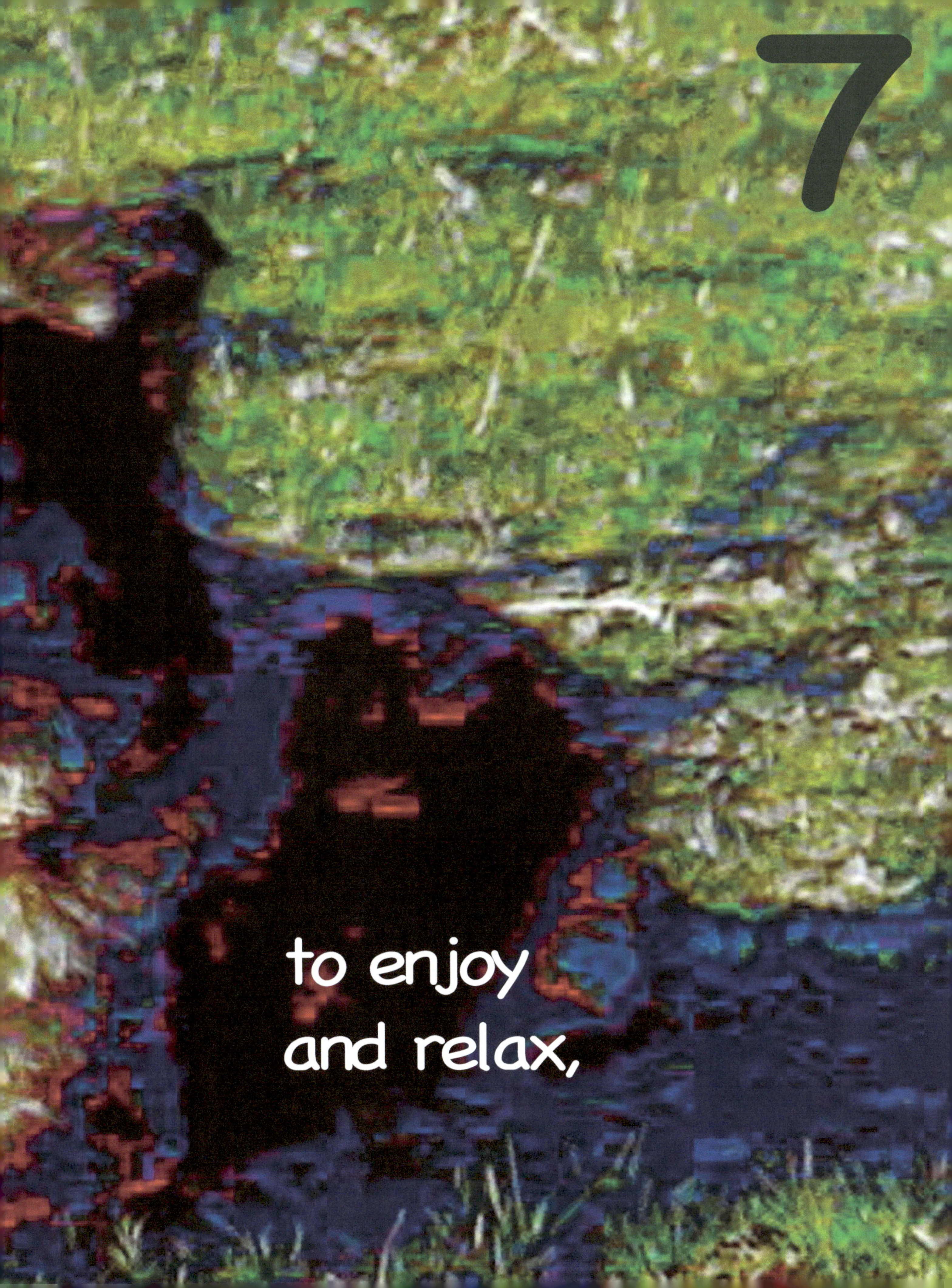

to enjoy
and relax,

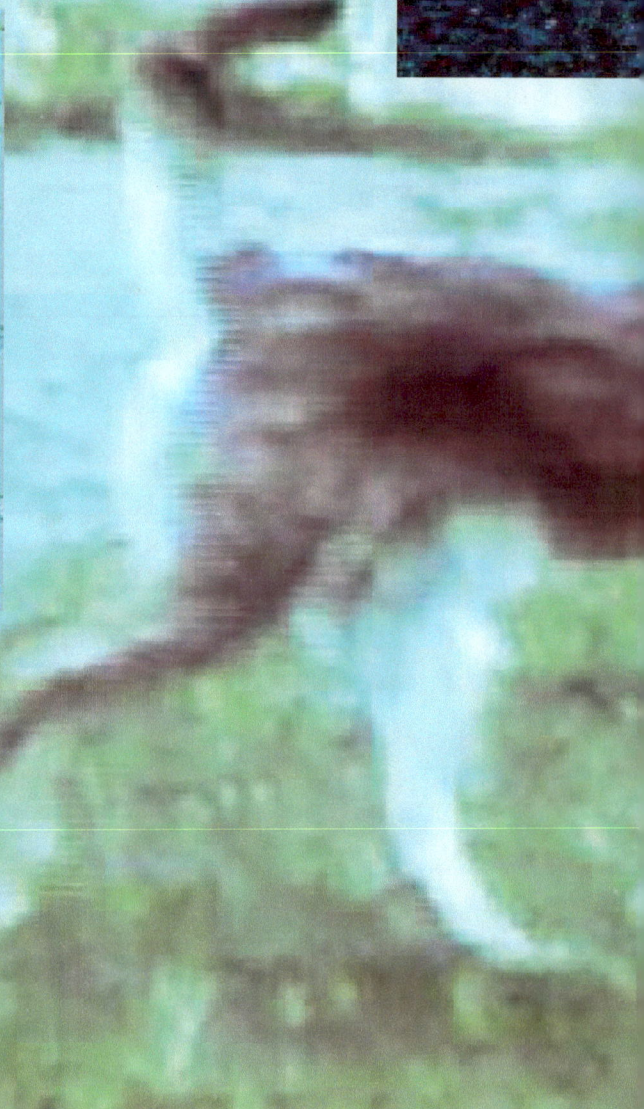

8

to explore

and have
challenging
adventures,

9

10

to play
with
new friends

and have fun.

The dog knows what I am going to do even before I know!

12

And he knows
when we sleep
and dream
we can reconnect
upward

and decide to visit
the land of the dogs,

stretched across
all time and space.

15

There is a man
in that land
who looks after
all the dogs,
and who put
the blue collar
on Ralph
so he would know
which one Ralph was.

Then Ralph wakes
and comes back.

6721

And if
the universe
knows
who my dog is,
it also sees him
right here
beside me.